IN DEEP WITH THE Octopus

by NORMA DIXON

Published in Canada by Fitzhenry & Whiteside,
195 Allstate Parkway, Markham, Ontario L3R 4T8

Published in the United States by Fitzhenry & Whiteside,
311 Washington Street, Brighton, Massachusetts 02135

www.fitzhenry.ca   godwit@fitzhenry.ca

10 9 8 7 6 5 4 3 2 1

Library and Archives Canada Cataloguing in Publication

Dixon, Norma
In deep with the octopus / by Norma Dixon.
Includes bibliographical references and index.

ISBN 978-1-55455-270-2
1. Octopuses--Juvenile literature. I. Title. II. Title: Octopus.
QL430.3.O2D59 2013   j594'.56   C2013-901846-8

Publisher Cataloging-in-Publication Data (U.S.)
Dixon, Norma.
In deep with the octopus / Norma Dixon.
[ ] p. : col. photos. ; cm.
Includes bibliographical references and index.

Summary: A journey inside the octopus's world, with facts, photos and
other information about the octopus—types, anatomy, life and
mating cycles, habitats, behavior, and intelligence.

ISBN-13: 978-1-55455-270-2
1. Octopuses -- Juvenile literature. I. Title.
594.56 [E] dc23 QL430.3.O2D596In 2013

Fitzhenry & Whiteside acknowledges with thanks the Canada Council for the Arts,
and the Ontario Arts Council for their support of our publishing program.
We acknowledge the financial support of the Government of Canada
through the Canada Book Fund (CBF) for our publishing activities.

Cover and interior design by Tanya Montini

Cover image © Planctonvideo, via Dreamstime.com

Printed in China by Sheck Wah Tong Printing Press Ltd.

Canada Council   Conseil des arts
for the Arts   du Canada

ONTARIO ARTS COUNCIL
CONSEIL DES ARTS DE L'ONTARIO
50 YEARS OF ONTARIO GOVERNMENT SUPPORT OF THE ARTS
50 ANS DE SOUTIEN DU GOUVERNEMENT DE L'ONTARIO AUX ARTS

IN DEEP WITH THE
Octopus

by NORMA DIXON

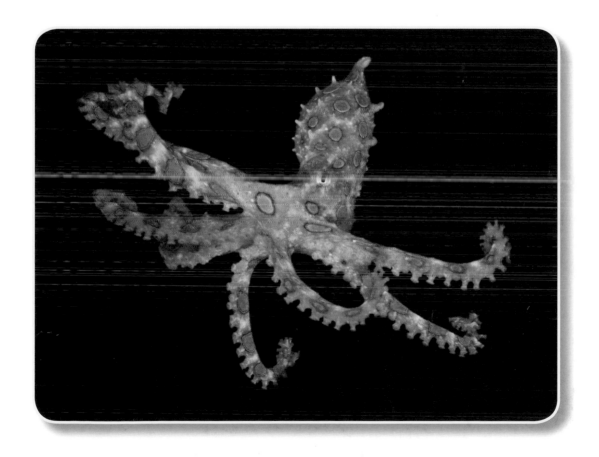

Fitzhenry & Whiteside

With thanks to Dorothy, Lisa and Nora.

A grateful acknowledgement goes to Heather Ylitalo-Ward,
PhD candidate in the Department of Zoology
at the University of Hawai`i at Manoa,
for providing meaningful insight into
the world of octopuses.

CONTENTS

INTRODUCTION   6

"Help!" Shrieks the Beautiful Heroine…
Folklore
Paul the Prophesying Octopus

**CHAPTER 1:
INSIDE OUT**   8

Blue Bloods
All-In-One Package
What's for Dinner?
Slowpokes of the Past
Arms that Think
Made of Muscle
Eight Arms, Always

**CHAPTER 2:
OCTOPUS SPECIALTIES**   12

Smarter than Fido?
Jet-Propelled Travellers
Chomp! Drill! Pull!
A Secret Weapon
20/20 Vision
Superior Senses
…With One Sense Missing

**CHAPTER 3:
ESCAPE ARTISTS**   14

A Bonus of Being Boneless
Camouflage Experts
Who's That?

**CHAPTER 4:
FROM EGG TO END**   16

Home Sweet Home
Making More Octopuses
An Unbelievable Pair
Dutiful Mothers
Octopuses Die Young

**CHAPTER 5:
ALL IN THE FAMILY**   19

The Killer
The Smallest
The Biggest
Oceans of Octopuses

**CHAPTER 6:
DANGER FOR ALL SEA LIFE** 28

Pollution Kills—Slowly and Silently
A Double Threat
An Octopus Omen

**CHAPTER 7:
WHAT DO YOU THINK?**   32

Octopus Wrestling, Anyone?
Octopus on Ice
Who Eats Octopuses?
Live Octopus Dish
Pet-able?
What Do You Know?

ARE YOU ARTISTIC?   36
GLOSSARY   37
INDEX   38
FURTHER READING   39
BIBLIOGRAPHY   39
IMAGE CREDITS   40

"HELP!"

Shrieks the Beautiful Heroine...

...as she is about to be torn to pieces and eaten by a huge, black, eight-armed creature that has emerged from the sea. Most of us have seen movies or comics with scenes like this. For years octopus-type monsters have been portrayed as ruthless killers. In *20,000 Leagues Under the Sea*, by Jules Verne, a huge octopus attacks the submarine *Nautilus*. You can watch an octopus wreck a whole city in the old movie *Tentacles of the Deep*, and see one gobble up passengers on a cruise ship in *Deep Rising*. We know that fictional monster-octopuses are created for thrills and chills, but it's easy to transfer the creepy feelings to real octopuses, and this has given them an unearned reputation as villains.

The hidden lives of octopuses in their underwater world is a mystery to many people. If you ask someone to describe an octopus, chances are, the first thing they will say is, "It has eight legs" or "It's a monster!" They might also add that it's slimy and dangerous and just waiting to grab an unsuspecting diver. Some people might think an octopus would make an interesting pet that they could keep as easily as a goldfish. There are lots of wrong ideas out there. However, you'll soon discover that these creatures are really clever, cunning, sensitive, and timid. You'll also find they have some crazy features, like taste buds on their arms, and some "yuck" habits, like slurping crab guts. What's more, you'll "out-know" people who say octopuses have eight legs. You can tell them, smugly, "Not so. Octopuses don't have any legs. They have eight arms."

The Cthulhu first appeared in H.P Lovecraft's "The Call of the Cthulhu." Described as a monster, the Cthulhu has a rubbery body, an octopus head and an unknown number of tentacles surrounding its mouth.

Folklore

Legend claims that an octopus built the Hawaiian islands by pushing up rocks from the ocean floor. Hawaiians also tell tales that the octopus is the sole survivor of a whole series of previous alien universes. Do you think this is possible?

Nootka people say Octopus was a woman with hair twisted into eight braids. One day, when she was digging clams at the edge of the sea, she was repeatedly pestered by Raven. She grew angry and suddenly changed her eight braids into long arms. She attached four arms to a rock and grabbed Raven with the other four. He struggled to free himself but Octopus held him tight. Soon the tide came in and covered them both. Raven drowned. The next day, he was miraculously rescued and brought back to life by his friend Crow. He never annoyed Octopus again.

Paul the Prophesying Octopus

No one knows how he did it. Paul was just an ordinary octopus (*Octopus vulgaris*) who came from the sea near Weymouth, England, to live in a tank in Oberhausen, Germany. He became internationally famous when he correctly predicted the winner of all seven games of Germany's 2010 FIFA World Cup for soccer, plus the final match winner. He then went on to correctly predict Spain's victory over the Netherlands in the 2010 World Cup Final. Paul performed his predictions by choosing which of two mussels he ate first. He was given two boxes, each holding a mussel. Each box was marked with the flag of a country that would be competing in the game. Somehow, the mussel Paul found most appetizing was always inside the box of the future winner.

Paul retired after his World Cup prediction and died the following October at about 2 years of age, the average lifespan for his species.

First Nations people on the Pacific Coast called octopuses "devil fish" and considered them vicious monsters.

When faced with the option of picking one of the boxes marked with the flags of Germany and Spain in the semi-finals of the 2010 FIFA World Cup, Paul correctly picked Spain as the winner.

CHAPTER 1

Inside Out

Would you like to meet an octopus? You can find one in any ocean in the world, but you might have to look carefully. You could snorkel right over one, or dive down beside one without seeing it because in seconds, an octopus can change its colours to match the background.

Over 300 kinds of octopuses roam the seafloor. Some are smaller than your hand, while others weigh over 200 pounds! And believe it or not, the bigger the octopus, the more timid it is. Whatever its size, an octopus would rather flee than fight.

You might think octopuses are ugly, but looks aren't everything. Octopuses are the smartest of all **invertebrates**. Meet a few of these tricksters and see how they can squirt ink, perform a disappearing act, and even come to recognize you.

An octopus could befriend you!

Invertebrate: Any creature that doesn't have a backbone. Other invertebrates include worms, snails, and caterpillars.

ONE OCTOPUS PLUS ONE OCTOPUS EQUALS WHAT?

Would you say two octopuses, octopi, octopae, or octopodes? All of them are right—well, a couple of them are kind of outdated. Most people go for "octopuses" so that's what we'll use in this book.

WHAT DO YOU KNOW?

1. What is a radula?
2. What does cephalopod mean?
3. What is melanin?
4. Why is the greater blue-ringed octopus deadly?
5. Why does an octopus have blue blood?
6. How does an octopus change directions?
7. Does an octopus have any hard parts?
8. How does an octopus prepare to eat a crab?

See page 35 for answers.

BLUE BLOODS

An octopus has blue blood and three hearts. Two of the three hearts work at pumping blood through two **gills** to pick up oxygen from the water, while the third heart pumps blood through the body.

Our blood is red because it's made up of **iron**. Octopus blood is blue because it is based on **copper**. Even with three hearts pumping, an octopus can get tired easily because blue blood is not good at carrying oxygen. This weakness is a bonus for the predators that chase them.

ALL-IN-ONE PACKAGE

You can't tell an octopus's head from its body because both are enclosed in one pulpy sac. The sac is covered with a tough membrane called the **mantle**, which holds all the octopus's inner workings. This is where you'll find the main brain, central nervous system, three hearts, breathing system, and all the intestines needed for digestion and getting rid of wastes.

Beneath the mantle is a watery space called the **mantle cavity**, which holds blood vessels and gills for breathing. An octopus absorbs oxygen into its bloodstream from water flowing through its gills. The water passes into the mantle cavity, then gets pushed out through a multi-use funnel called a **siphon** that shoots ink, eliminates waste, and creates jet propulsion.

When an octopus eats, the food travels through the **esophagus** where it is mixed with saliva. Then it travels into a **crop**, a kind of pouch, where it is further digested before it passes into the stomach. Digestive juices break down the food completely, sending nourishment to the bloodstream and waste to the kidneys.

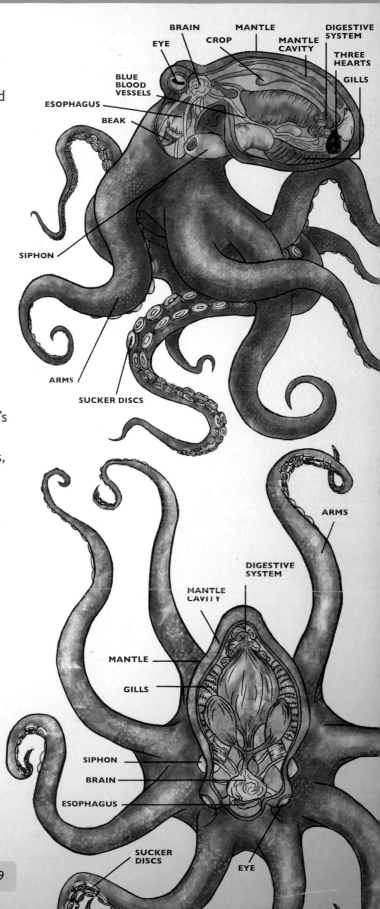

9

An octopus eats a crab whole.

A typical octopus diet.

Killer whale

Seals

Narwhal

Moray eel

WHAT'S FOR DINNER?

If you enjoy eating all kinds of seafood, you have lots in common with octopuses. Octopuses don't count calories. If they are in the mood for food, which is most of the time, they eat just about anything they can catch. Bottom-dwelling octopuses eat mainly crabs, sea worms, whelks and clams. Those that live in the open ocean go for prawns, fish, and their cousin squids or even other octopuses. They will also spread out on the seafloor, trolling with their **sucker discs** for microscopic **plankton** "soup." Hungry octopuses have also been known to climb over the sides of fishing boats and eat the catch!

Octopuses contribute to the food chain by becoming meals for moray eels, sea stars, narwhals, seals and whales. They are also eaten by people.

SLOWPOKES OF THE PAST

Octopuses we see today are as different from their ancestors as log rafts are from speed boats. Ages ago, octopuses wore shells and moved slowly across the ocean floor where they became meals for larger fish. Those that managed to survive the longest were the ones that had the smallest shells because they could move around faster. Over many centuries, the shells on each new generation of survivors became smaller and smaller, until finally, they disappeared completely. Once their shells vanished, their soft bodies became tough and muscular. Gradually, they became the wily, free-swimming octopuses we know today.

ARMS THAT THINK

Try patting your head and rubbing your stomach at the same time. Did you rub your head and pat your stomach? We have a hard time making our two arms perform separate tasks at the same time, but an octopus can make each of its eight arms perform a different task, all at once! Each arm gets directions from its own nerve cluster, or mini-brain, located where the arm joins the body. All the main brain has to do is think in a general sort of way; for example, "I'm hungry." Then each mini-brain takes over, telling its arm, "Grab that fish!" or "Open that clam!" and each arm acts on its own. The arm tips also work together to do complicated things like unwrapping packages, or perform delicate tasks like picking the meat out of a crab leg or probing cracks and crevices to feel for hidden prey.

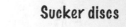

Sucker discs

MADE OF MUSCLES

Could you drag a tractor? With a lot of effort, humans can drag an object that's twice their own weight. An octopus, on the other hand, can drag an object that's 20 times its own weight! Each of its 8 rubbery arms has 10 muscles and 2 rows of strong sucker discs. That's 80 muscles and about 1,500 sucker discs in all. Each disc acts like a strong, sensitive suction cup. If just one of those suction cups latched onto you, you'd have a hard time prying it off.

EIGHT ARMS, ALWAYS

If an enemy rips off an octopus's arm, a whole new arm, complete with a mini-brain, will grow in its place. Here's the really strange thing—the torn-off arm will stay alive because it will still be getting orders from its mini-brain. No one seems to know how long the separated arm can last without a body, but in the wild, it would probably be quickly gobbled up for someone's dinner.

CHAPTER 2

Octopus Specialties

SMARTER THAN FIDO?

Octopuses are such a brainy bunch that some researchers think they are smarter than dogs. If you were friends with an octopus, it would come to know you. It might even squirt you with water to get your attention, or miss you and mope around if you were away. Octopuses can even recognize and distinguish shapes. They can find their way through a maze by checking landmarks, and if you take away the landmarks, they can still get through by memorizing the route. Octopuses can also be copy cats. They can learn to perform tasks like opening jars and turning on taps by watching other octopuses.

An octopus will accept food from your hand if you're brave enough to offer it.

A typical transportation style: moving head first with arms trailing behind.

JET-PROPELLED TRAVELLERS

You'd have a tough time keeping up with a swimming octopus. These creatures are water powered, and they zip along head first, trailing their arms behind them. They swim by drawing water through the openings behind their eyes and shooting it out through a rear funnel. The force of the ejected water propels them along, and when they want to change directions, their funnel opening swings around like a fire hose. They can also travel at top speed when they're crawling over the seabed.

CHOMP! DRILL! PULL!

An octopus has ways of getting its dinner out of the hardest shell. You'll find a mouth where its eight arms meet, but it doesn't look like a mouth. It looks like the kind of sharp, curved beak you'd expect to see on a parrot. The beak is made of tough stuff called **chitin** (kahy-tin), which is the same material our fingernails are made of. It's the only hard part of an octopus's rubbery body. One bite from its beak will crack the shell of a crab or lobster. Inside the beak is a tongue-like organ called a **radula** (raj-a-la), which is covered with rows of teeth as fine as sandpaper. When the octopus wants to make a hole in a shell, the radula works like a combined drill and scraper.

An octopus's mouth is located where its eight arms meet.

A SECRET WEAPON

When an octopus is being sneaky, it watches from behind a rock until a crab or lobster comes crawling across the seafloor. Then it quickly spreads out above the small prey like an open umbrella, lands on top of it and wraps it in a deadly embrace. Next, the octopus uses its beak to crack the crab's shell. Then, it squirts its secret weapon into the opening—poisonous spit! The spit will either turn the crab's insides into gloop, which the octopus will suck out, or else it will paralyze the crab so it can't move while being eaten.

All octopuses have venomous spit and there's a possibility that some could kill a human with their bite, but this has never been proven satisfactorily. Only the greater blue-ringed octopus is known for sure to have a bite that is fatal to humans, and it only bites if it's provoked.

20/20 VISION

When you watch an octopus, it can watch you back. It can see you very clearly because its eyes are a lot like ours. The pupils grow bigger or smaller to let in more or less light, allowing the octopus to see sharp images and focus on something as small as a grain of sand 1 metre (3 ft) away. This sharp vision is a big help when hunting. Underwater researchers say they often get a creepy feeling that while they're studying an octopus, the octopus appears to be studying them too!

Octopuses might have great eye sight, but they're also colour blind. Light waves do all the work.

A reef octopus hiding behind a rock, waiting for its prey to come by.

SUPERIOR SENSES

Imagine being able to taste with your arms or your forehead. All our taste buds are in our mouth, but an octopus has taste receptors all over its body, making it as much as 1,000 times more sensitive to taste than humans. Most taste receptors are located in the octopus's sucker discs and arm tips, so it can taste while it touches. It can also smell as it touches. Each arm tip has scent detectors that are linked to a smell centre, located in two small pits behind the eyes. This gives an octopus the advantage of having eight "noses."

Octopus eyes have rectangular pupils.

...WITH ONE SENSE MISSING

No matter how much noise you make, an octopus won't hear you. It has no ears and is completely deaf. Don't try to sneak up on one though; it can still sense vibrations of sound under water.

CHAPTER 3

Now you see it—blink—and it's gone.

Escape Artists

If you happen to dive down and scare an octopus, you could face a blast of black ink. An upset octopus can turn its funnel your way, shoot out a jet of ink, and leave you staring at a black cloud. Squirting ink is a trick an octopus uses to escape from predators. While the confused enemy is trying to find its way in the dark, the octopus performs a disappearing act and gets away. The ink can be more than a smokescreen, too. It can irritate a predator's eyes and affect its sense of smell. An octopus that lives in a small space, like an aquarium tank, can be harmed by its own ink if the water isn't continually changed.

Some octopuses also shoot out **false bodies**. When their ink is mixed with mucous, it forms a cloud similar in shape and size to the octopus's body. While the predator goes for the phantom, the real octopus jets away to safety. The inky mucous takes a long time to dissolve; it will drift around in gauzy grey threads until it sinks.

*Octopus ink contains **melanin**, the same pigment or colouring agent that gives you the colour of your skin and hair. In ancient times, melanin was taken directly out of octopuses' ink-producing glands and used for writing.*

A BONUS OF BEING BONELESS
An octopus can squeeze its boneless body into crevices so narrow that a hungry enemy could never reach it. You can imagine how this flexible creature gets through small openings if you think of squeezing a plastic bag full of jelly through a knot hole. You wouldn't try cramming it through all at once, but feeding it through just a little bit at a time. The only part of an octopus that is not flexible is its beak. If the beak can get through an opening, so can the rest of the octopus.

CAMOUFLAGE EXPERTS
Wouldn't it be handy if you could suddenly disappear against the wallpaper? An octopus can vanish by matching its colour to the background. It can pull off this sneaky trick because its skin contains zillions of microscopic pigment sacs— about 200 sacs per square millimetre. These sacs are called **chromatophores** (cro-*mat*-o-fors). They are all connected to a tiny set of muscles. Each chromatophore sac contains red, yellow, blue, brown or black pigment. When the sacs expand or constrict, they show more of their colours. The pigments

An octopus's body is boneless.

match themselves to their surrounding colours by responding to the patterns of light waves. An octopus will change colours when it's angry or scared, or when it wants to show off for a female or a rival male. Many can also change the texture of their skin by raising bumps or spikes to suddenly look like coral or seaweed.

If you put an octopus in an aquarium tank next to a tank full of fish, you'd better make sure there is no pipe joining the two tanks. The octopus might manage to squeeze through the pipe and it would be "goodbye fish."

Can you make out the octopus? It's camouflaged on the Mediterranean seabed.

WHO'S THAT?

If you see a mimic octopus *(Thaumoctopus mimicus)* that isn't in disguise, it'll look like a regular octopus with a brown-and-white pattern and an arm span up to 60 cm (2 ft) across. But startle it, and it might "transform" into one of the other sea creatures of the Malaysian Archipelago. If the mimic octopus wants to look like a poisonous flatfish that few others want to eat, it arranges its arms in a leaf shape, changes its colour to match the seabed, and swims away flatfish-style by rippling its flexible body. Sometimes, damsel fish, which are only about three inches long, will gang up to attack an octopus. But a mimic octopus will scare these predators off by sticking six of its eight arms into a hole and leaving the remaining two arms free to wave back and forth. Now it looks like a sea snake that eats damsel fish. Other tricks include cruising along with its arms sticking out in all directions so it will be mistaken for a dangerous lion fish waving venomous spines, or floating near the surface with its arms stretched above its body, acting like a huge stinging anemone. The mimic octopus also imitates the colours and movements of the brittle star, giant crab, sting ray, flounder, jelly fish and mantis shrimp.

The mimic octopus is a fast-moving shape shifter.

Thanks to their pigment sacs, octopuses can change colours in a jiffy, like this bright blue octopus.

15

CHAPTER 4

From Egg to End

HOME SWEET HOME

Octopuses make themselves at home in all the world's oceans, tropical to icy. You can find them in shallow tidal pools and down to a depth of 762 metres (2,500 ft). You won't find them in any fresh water though.

If octopuses could hang Private Property signs on their lairs, they would. These guys are loners that don't like sharing. They're good at finding hiding places with room for just one. You might find a small octopus with its body squeezed into a pop can or Styrofoam cup that someone has tossed into the sea. In the tropics where people throw out coconut shells, octopuses often curl up in half a shell then pull the other half over the top. Sometimes, they will hide behind barricades they have made from rocks and debris.

When an octopus makes a den, it clears the sand and pebbles from a crack or crevice so it can squeeze inside. If you see a pile of fish bones and empty shells on the seafloor, it could mean a hidden octopus has done some housekeeping by pushing all its garbage out the door. Octopuses are also keen interior decorators. They often decorate their dens with stones, bottle caps and other gems they find on the seafloor.

Sorry, there's only room for one in here.

An octopus hiding in a bottle.

Although a seemingly simple task to us, manipulating a coconut shell to be used as a shelter requires a lot of complex thought. This intricate planning makes octopuses the first-ever invertebrates known to use tools.

MAKING MORE OCTOPUSES

Most octopuses are such loners it's a wonder they ever get together. They usually look so much alike that males can't be sure if they're near a possible girlfriend, or just another guy. An interested female will let a male sit beside her.

Many males can be identified by checking their arms. If the third right arm has a flattened tip devoid of sucker discs, you can be pretty sure you're looking at the macho

Wait...before we start dating, I have to ask—are you a girl?

type. Because this arm doesn't have chromatophores like the other seven arms, males often keep it curled up so it doesn't give away their camouflage disguises. The male uses the special arm to take a package of sperm from the sperm holder in its mantle cavity. Then it places the package in a sperm receptacle in the female's mantle cavity. This process takes just a few seconds, but the female often keeps the sperm in storage for almost a year before using it to fertilize her mature eggs.

People who study octopuses say these creatures are so bashful and solitary that it's hard to study their mating habits. Some males appear to simply pass the sperm packet to a receptive female with no ceremony, and others try to impress her by putting on a macho colour-changing act. A few types of males will even hang around to help a female guard her eggs.

Here! Take good care of this sperm package.

AN UNBELIEVABLE PAIR

Do you think a female octopus over 2 metres (6.5 ft) long and a male octopus about the size of a walnut could be attracted to each other? If they happen to be a pair of blanket octopuses (Tremoctopus), they could meet, mate, and be responsible for the production of 100,000 eggs. This twosome goes about mating much differently than other octopuses. When the male sees the lady of his dreams, he detaches a special arm that stores sperm. The arm swims toward the female, enters her mantle and fertilizes her eggs. But the romantic couple doesn't live happily ever after. Shortly after mating the male dies and the female lives just long enough to see her eggs hatch. Blanket octopuses get their name from the transparent webs between three of the arms on the adult female that spread out like a blanket when she swims.

DUTIFUL MOTHERS

Depending on the species, once a female octopus gets around to creating offspring, she can produce about 200,000 eggs in long strings, using mucous to cement them to hard surfaces. She watches over them, clearing them of sand, driving off predators, and sometimes spraying ink on would-be raiders. Though most of those 200,000 eggs will hatch, only about two of the hatchlings will survive to become adults. The rest become food for other ocean creatures.

The hatchlings are mini-versions of their parents. They spend the first few weeks of their lives drifting near the surface, eating microscopic plankton. Once its mantle has had a chance to grow, the hatchling will settle on the seafloor.

Baby octopuses look like mini-versions of their parents.

OCTOPUSES DIE YOUNG

Octopuses are programmed to die of starvation. During the one to three months that a female waits for her eggs to hatch, she never eats or leaves her den. Soon after the eggs hatch, she dies.

Both males and females have appetite-suppressing glands that go to work after mating. The **secretions** in the glands stop the octopuses from feeling hungry, so they don't hunt or eat. Usually, they grow so weak they get caught by predators before they starve to death.

The average lifespan of an octopus in the ocean is 2 years. Octopuses that are kept in aquarium tanks and never get the chance to mate can live for 5 or 6 years. Bigger species like the giant Pacific octopus can reach the age of 10.

This octopus mama is surrounded by her eggs.

CHAPTER 5

All in the Family

Do you look like your cousins? An octopus resembles its cousins because all octopuses look as if their feet grow right out of their heads! Their nearest relatives are squids, nautiluses and cuttlefish. They all share a Greek name, **cephalopod** (sef-al-o-pod), which means "head footed," but the Greeks goofed. Cephalopods don't actually have feet or legs. Their slithery tentacles are really arms, and the eight arms of an octopus have such sensitive tips that they actually act like fingers.

The octopus and its cousin cephalopods belong to a huge group of soft-bodied animals called **molluscs**, which includes squishy creatures like slugs, and shell-wearers like snails and oysters. Cephalopods are the smart clan of the mollusc group, and octopuses are the smartest of them all.

Copper kills octopuses. A penny tossed into a tank will not only kill the octopus but any other molluscs that live with it. Copper pipes can't even be used in octopus aquariums.

THE KILLER

(Hapalochlaena lunulata) One bite from the greater blue-ringed octopus and you're a goner, unless you get immediate mouth-to-mouth resuscitation. This little octopus is only the size of a golf ball, but its toxic saliva holds a nerve poison that quickly stops unlucky victims from breathing. Its beak is even sharp enough to pierce a diver's wetsuit. The blue-ringed is the only octopus with a bite that's fatal to humans, but fortunately, it won't attack unless it's being pestered. You can identify this small killer by the pattern of blue rings all over its body. When it's aggravated its rings glow brighter, warning would-be attackers, "I'm poisonous, back off!" This scary critter can be found in the Pacific and Indian Oceans, from Japan to Australia.

Small and pretty with a deadly bite.

THE SMALLEST

(Octopus wolfi) Here's one that could hide under a penny! The star-sucker pygmy octopus measures just 1.5 cm (3/5 in) and weighs less than a gram. If you look closely, you can identify males by the unusual fringed rims on their suckers. These mini-molluscs live in the warm waters of the Indo-Pacific Ocean. Though they were first discovered in 1913, scientists have only just recently begun to study their habits.

Another competitor for the "smallest" title is the California Lilliput octopus *(Octopus micropyrsus)*. The Lilliput measures from about 1 cm to 1.5 cm (approx. 2/5 to 3/5 in), and like the star-sucker pygmy octopus, its lifestyle is still a mystery.

THE BIGGEST

(Enteroctopus dofleini) This one could fill your bedroom! The giant Pacific octopus can weigh over 90 kg (200 lbs) and have an arm-spread of over 10 m (30 ft). This monster is very shy, but it has earned a bad reputation because of its curiosity about divers. It likes to swim alongside them and run an exploring arm over their masks and bodies. If the diver stays calm, the octopus will swim away with its curiosity satisfied, but if the diver panics and tries to pull the arm from his face, the octopus will cling tighter and the diver could drown.

Most of these giants live off the coast of British Columbia, but some stray farther north or south. They eat all kinds of seafood and sometimes birds or seals, but so far, there have been no signs of them eating people for lunch.

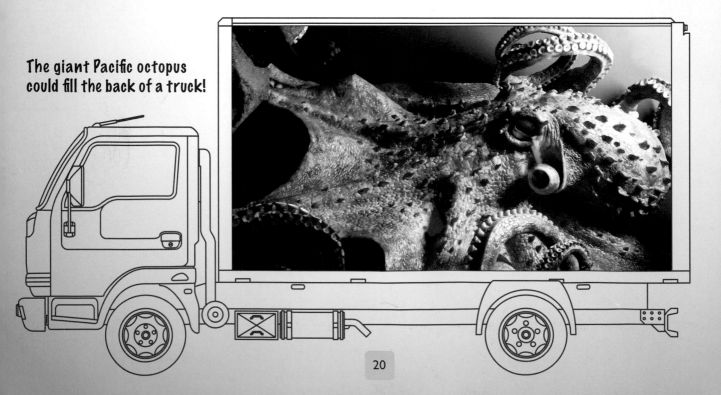

The giant Pacific octopus could fill the back of a truck!

Oceans of Octopuses

Octopuses don't tend to stay in one location. Often, you'll find a few of the species that thrive in Malaysia living on the Great Barrier Reef, or a Gulf of Mexico resident turning up in the Caribbean. And the common octopus? Well, that one you'll find almost anywhere.

OCEANS WORLDWIDE

The Common Octopus (Octopus vulgaris)

This is your "classic" octopus. It's the most studied of all octopus species. You can find it settled off the coast of England, living comfortably in the Mediterranean Sea, or being caught by the trawler-load around West Africa. It's also at home in the frigid Bering Sea and the warm water of the Indian Ocean. You'll find it in the Pacific Ocean—from the Sea of Japan, east to Alaska, and south to California. It can grow to have a 25 cm (9.8 in) mantle and arms up to 1 metre (3 ft) long.

PACIFIC OCEAN

Wonderpus Octopus (Wunderpus photogenicus)

Wonderpus—a name for a clever cat? No. The "pus" in wonderpus is short for "octopus" not for "puss." Wonderpus is a wonder in the octopus world because of its unique markings. No two of these creatures look alike. Scientists can keep track of an individual by the pattern of spots on its body and the stripes on its legs. Wonderpus prefers to hunt in the twilight hours of dawn and dusk, in the shallow waters of Malaysia and Indonesia. Its body is small—only about 7.3 cm (approx. 3 in) and its arms are about 7 times longer than its body. Wonderpus was first spotted in the 1980s but has only recently been described by scientists.

The first reported albino octopus was recently found on the dark seafloor in Antarctica.

Don't be fooled by the extremely endangered Pacific Northwest tree octopus. It began showing up on the Internet in 1998 with pictures of the creature high up among tree branches. The octopus and the pictures are a hoax created by a guy named Lyle Zapato.

Wonderpus octopus

Here are some places where you can usually find a few different types of octopuses:

BERING SEA AND WEST COAST OF CANADA
Giant Pacific Octopus
Enteroctopus dofleini

ATLANTIC OCEAN
Atlantic Longarm Octopus
Octopus defilippi

ATLANTIC OCEAN, CARIBBEAN TO CAPE CANAVERAL
Atlantic Pygmy Octopus
Octopus joubini

GULF OF MEXICO
Four-eyed Octopus
Octopus maya

PACIFIC OCEAN, HAWAII TO EAST COAST OF AFRICA
Big Blue Octopus (Day Octopus)
Octopus cyanea

CARIBBEAN SEA
Caribbean Reef Octopus
Octopus briareus

ATLANTIC OCEAN, AFRICAN COAST
Dumbo Octopus
Grimpoteuthis

PACIFIC OCEAN
Wonderpus Octopus
Wunderpus photogenicus

Transparent Pelagic Octopus
Vitreledonella richardi

ANTARCTIC OCEAN
Turquet's Octopus
Pareledone turqueti

ARCTIC OCEAN
Northern Common Octopus
Octopus vulgaris

**OCEANS
WORLDWIDE**
Common Octopus
Octopus vulgaris

MEDITERRANEAN SEA
Common Octopus
Octopus vulgaris

**WESTERN AND
NORTHERN PACIFIC**
Giant Pacific Octopus
Octopus dofleini

MALAYSIA

INDIAN OCEAN
Coconut Octopus
Amphioctopus marginatus

A coconut octopus
toting its shell.

**COASTAL WATERS
OF AUSTRALIA**
Banded Drop-arm Octopus
Ameloctopus litoralis

**GREAT
BARRIER
REEF**

TASMAN SEA
Blanket Octopus
Tremoctopus violaceus

23

Transparent
pelagic octopus

Atlantic
longarm octopus

Transparent Pelagic Octopus (*Vitreledonella richardi*)
You can see right through it! This octopus is gelatinous, transparent, and almost invisible and colourless. It can be found deep down in tropical and subtropical waters. This octopus is so rare that it's seldom ever seen and scientists still have to catch one before they can study its inner workings. In April 2012 though, one was spotted out of the window of a DeepSee submersible, almost 180 m (590 ft) down in the ocean. Photos of the transparent pelagic octopus show that the only opaque parts of its body are its eyes and digestive gland. These appear only as shadows to enemies looking up at the octopus as it swims against lighted water. Do you think a transparent octopus would need to camouflage itself like other octopuses? Could we see what it ate for dinner? Can it squirt ink? As soon as specialists discover its secrets, they'll send out the news.

ARCTIC OCEAN

Northern Common Octopus (*Octopus vulgaris*)
This common octopus lives where it can't get much colder. Usually it inhabits warm and temperate waters, but changes in its bodily makeup and DNA have produced a protein that insulates it from the frigid water. So, it has been able to adapt to life near the North Pole. Scientists have studied its stomach contents and found remains of squid, flatfish and snow crabs that live at the bottom of icy seas. This Arctic octopus's worst enemy is the narwhal.

ATLANTIC OCEAN

Atlantic Longarm Octopus (*Octopus defilippi*)
"Longarm" is right! This great imitator has arms that are seven times longer than its body. It quickly arranges those arms, and presto! It looks like a flounder, or a starfish, or whichever disguise it needs to fool an enemy. Usually, it's brown with small white spots, but its colour and texture can change in seconds. Its eyes are high up on its head with a bump over each one. Fully grown, its body and arms together can be about 1 metre (3.2 ft) long. Instead of laying eggs in strings like most other female octopuses, female longarms carry their eggs under their mantles until they hatch. Longarms are found in the coral reefs of Australia, Malta, and the Florida Keys, where they hunt at night for the crabs that make up most of their diet.

Dumbo
octopus

ATLANTIC OCEAN, AFRICAN COAST
Dumbo Octopus *(Grimpoteuthis)*
Dumbo octopuses aren't dumb. They get their name because they look like Disney's Dumbo, the flying elephant. Dumbo the elephant can fly by flapping its big ears. Dumbo the octopus, on the other hand, swims by waving two big ear-like fins that protrude from the top of its head. It also gets around like other octopuses by jet propulsion. Dumbos are among the rarest octopuses. They live at extreme depths of the ocean, down as deep as 7 kilometres (4.35 miles). When they are on the seabed, they feast on worms and crustaceans, and when they are swimming, they eat mostly very small crustaceans called copepods. While other octopuses chew their food, Dumbos swallow their prey whole. The largest recorded Dumbo was 1.8 metres (approx. 6 ft) long.

INDIAN OCEAN
Coconut Octopus *(Amphioctopus marginatus)*
Their name might be nutty but these guys are actually pretty clever. They work very hard to dig coconut shells out of the sand, and then carry them around to reassemble as instant houses and hiding places. However, it's *how* they carry their shells that's really strange. The coconut octopus's body size is about 8 cm (approx. 3 in), and its arms are about 15 cm (5.9 in) long. When one of them stands over a couple of stacked coconut shells, its arms barely reach beneath. It lifts and holds the shells using some of its arms, then "tiptoes" over the seafloor on the tips of its free arms. It has even been seen walking on just two arms, making it a temporary **biped**. Divers say that when they see a coconut octopus lugging its load, they have a hard time stopping themselves from laughing. Most coconut octopuses live in the soft sediment in the waters around Indonesia where they can find a good supply of coconut shells.

After the coconut octopus buries itself under the sand, it uses a shell for protection.

CARIBBEAN SEA
Caribbean Reef Octopus *(Octopus briareus)*
It hunts by night. In turn, it's hunted by people with powerful searchlights. The blue-green skin of the Caribbean reef octopus reflects light,

A night hunter with unusual light-reflecting skin.

making it easy to spot as it seeks small fish and crustaceans among sea grasses and coral reefs. Female Caribbean reef octopuses lay fewer eggs than other octopuses—only about 500. The hatchlings emerge in a shorter time than those of other species and they can immediately swim, crawl and eject ink. Those that don't get eaten will mature and be ready to start their own families in about 145 days. Most Caribbean reef octopuses average about 100 cm (30.5 ft) long, including their arms. Like other octopuses, they can change their skin colour and texture to hide from enemies.

ANTARCTIC OCEAN

Turquet's Octopus (*Pareledone turqueti*)
These ocean-floor dwellers are stay-at-home octopuses. They hang around their own territory and move only to escape their most-feared enemies, Patagonian toothfish and Weddell seals. The Turquet's can be found all around the icy seas of Antarctica, both in shallow water and down as deep as 1,000 metres (3,280 feet). Most Turquet's octopuses have a mantle that is about 15 cm (5.9 in) long and skin that's covered with granular bumps. They eat from a plentiful supply of marine creatures that are at home in the frigid water, including crabs, shrimps, and sea snails.

GULF OF MEXICO

Four-eyed Octopus (*Octopus maya*)
The four-eyed octopus has only two eyes. Some specimens have spots that look like extra eyes, but most do not. No other octopus is quite like this one. It's exclusive to the waters off the coast of Yucatán, and has been declared a separate species. For years it has been caught and eaten by Mexican fishermen, and it's so popular that restrictions have been placed on the number that can be hauled in.

Atlantic pygmy octopus

Turquet's octopus

Four-eyed octopus

ATLANTIC OCEAN, CARIBBEAN TO CAPE CANAVERAL

<u>Atlantic Pygmy Octopus</u> *(Octopus joubini)*
It's small but it can do everything the big boys can. The Atlantic pygmy octopus squirts ink, changes colours, and drills holes in clam shells. It can also paralyze its victims with poisonous spit. When it rests or hides, it uses empty bivalve shells, pop cans or tiny crevices. It likes to "shut the door" on its shelter by pulling something into the opening. Fully grown, these minis are just 4.5 cm (1.75 in) long, with arms up to 9 cm (3.5 in long). Their menus mostly consist of small crustaceans.

PACIFIC OCEAN, HAWAII TO EAST COAST OF AFRICA

<u>Big Blue Octopus (Day Octopus)</u> *(Octopus cyanea)*
It's a mystery why this mostly brown octopus is often called the big blue. It has a light-coloured false eye at the base of its arms, but when it changes colours to camouflage itself, the eye disappears. Big blues capture crabs, poison them, and carry them home to eat. Their other food sources are found among coral reefs where they catch fish and other creatures that destroy algae. Because corals need algae to stay healthy, big blue octopuses are an important part of the reef community. These octopuses can grow to have a 16 cm (6.3 in) mantle with arms up to 80 cm (2.75 in long). They are widespread in the southern Pacific Ocean and can be found off the North Coast of Australia. It is the most common octopus to be eaten in Hawaii.

This coral-reef saver eats reef destroyers.

Eye a Squid, Ogle an Octopus

Squids and octopuses have a lot in common. Both have hard beaks, squirt ink, and are experts at camouflage. Their inner workings are much the same with blue blood and three hearts. Both squids and octopuses can look at you with very developed eyes. Compare these cousins though, and you'll see the squid's head-body combo looks firm, while the octopus looks blobby. Count a squid's arms and you might say "10." Check again and you'll see 2 are longer than the other 8. These aren't arms; they're actually specialized tentacles used to reach out and grab prey. Squids are also more sociable than octopuses. Though they live in the open ocean, they frequently travel in schools, and often mate in large groups. Octopuses are solitary creatures that live in dens on the ocean floor and mate very privately.

CHAPTER 6

Danger for All Sea Life

POLLUTION KILLS— SLOWLY AND SILENTLY

What would you do if someone dumped garbage in your yard? How would you act if you went to take a bath and found acid in the water? No doubt you would be angry and would quickly take steps to have things corrected. Octopuses are extremely sensitive creatures that are threatened by all kinds of changes to their environments. If **salinity** (salt content) in the water changes due to sewage runoff or fresh water being introduced to the system, most octopuses would likely die. When humans' lifestyles cause the ocean's temperature to rise and the water to become acidic, under-sea dwellers can't do anything but adapt or die. If they survive, they can be deformed or unable to reproduce.

The top few metres of the ocean store as much heat as the Earth's entire atmosphere, so as the planet warms, it's the ocean that gets most of the extra heat. The first casualties of a warmed-up ocean are plankton and **krill**. Plankton is a mix of tiny plants and animals that occupies a place right at the bottom of the food chain. It's eaten by newly hatched octopuses and fish, bivalves, and dozens of other creatures. In turn, plankton eaters provide food for bigger animals. Plant plankton is called phytoplankton. It makes food from sunlight, just like plants that grow in soil; it can't survive in polluted or overheated water. Dead plankton means no food for the creatures that eat it, and no food for those that eat the plankton eaters. Starvation could run right along the food chain until the finale—dead oceans.

Dumped junk makes a sick ocean.

Zooplankton is made up of tiny animals, while plant plankton is made up of microscopic plants.

Plankton dies when clouded or muddy water blocks the sun from entering the water.

Krill, a type of zooplankton, is made up of almost invisible shrimp-like creatures that breed in the coldest water, near sea ice. It's a food source for octopus hatchlings, fish and even blue and humpback whales. In parts of the ocean, rising temperatures have caused krill populations to drop by a staggering 80%, causing most of the fish in the area to disappear.

The ocean also holds about one quarter of the carbon dioxide we make from burning **fossil fuels** like coal, natural gas and oil. An overload of carbon dioxide will cause the water to become acidic, which prevents bivalves like clams and oysters from making strong shells. Thin, weak shells can't protect them and they die prematurely, taking a food source from other sea creatures like octopuses.

Ocean dwellers depend on us to save their world. We can start by cleaning up our own world of garbage or anything else that might end up in the oceans and harm the sea life.

A DOUBLE THREAT

Octopuses are being threatened by more than ocean warming. Some species are being overfished. The threat of **overfishing** occurs when too many sexually mature females are fished. Because female octopuses only lay eggs once and then die, those caught by fishermen would not have had a chance to lay eggs, therefore reducing the number of octopuses in the next year. Fortunately though, octopuses are smart and it seems that the females often avoid this fate by going into deeper waters to lay their eggs. Nonetheless, there is a potential for a crash if they are overfished.

Burning fossil fuels is harmful to our oceans.

Every year, up to 100,000 tons of the common octopus are taken out of the sea, mostly by commercial fishermen. These freshly caught octopuses are drying at a restaurant.

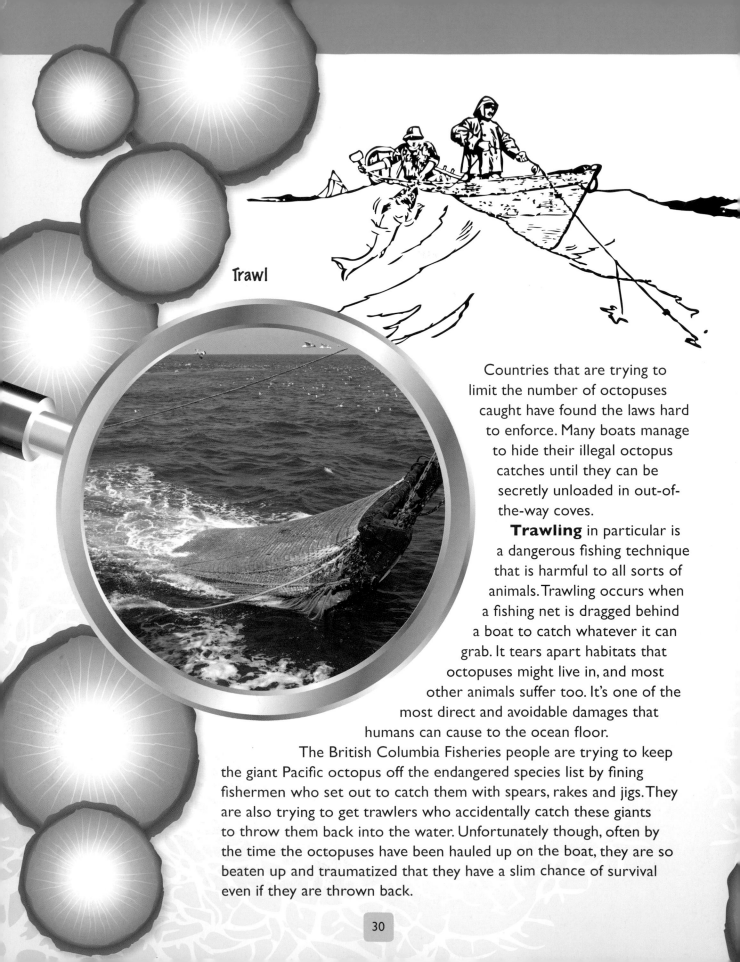

Trawl

Countries that are trying to limit the number of octopuses caught have found the laws hard to enforce. Many boats manage to hide their illegal octopus catches until they can be secretly unloaded in out-of-the-way coves.

Trawling in particular is a dangerous fishing technique that is harmful to all sorts of animals. Trawling occurs when a fishing net is dragged behind a boat to catch whatever it can grab. It tears apart habitats that octopuses might live in, and most other animals suffer too. It's one of the most direct and avoidable damages that humans can cause to the ocean floor.

The British Columbia Fisheries people are trying to keep the giant Pacific octopus off the endangered species list by fining fishermen who set out to catch them with spears, rakes and jigs. They are also trying to get trawlers who accidentally catch these giants to throw them back into the water. Unfortunately though, often by the time the octopuses have been hauled up on the boat, they are so beaten up and traumatized that they have a slim chance of survival even if they are thrown back.

AN OCTOPUS OMEN

When you look at a map of Antarctica, you'll notice that the ocean south of the Antarctic Circle is divided into the Weddell Sea and the Ross Sea. The two seas are separated by the West Antarctic Ice Sheet. The Turquet's octopus lives in both seas. These octopuses don't travel very much, and they move only to escape predators. Their habit of staying put made researchers think that, because the Weddell Sea and Ross Sea are entirely separate and on opposite sides of the Antarctic, each sea would have a different type of Turquet's octopus. However, when they studied the genes of Turquet's taken from both seas, they discovered their genes were almost identical.

Researchers say this could have happened only if centuries ago, when the climate was much warmer, the West Antarctic Ice Sheet collapsed to make the two seas into one. Then, over the centuries, the ice sheet reformed. But today it's no longer very stable. If **global warming** continues, the whole formation could collapse again. This ice collapse would result in a five-metre rise in the world's oceans, causing flooded coastlines and submerged islands.

The possible repetition of this threat to our planet was not revealed until researchers examined the Turquet's octopus.

The Antarctic Ocean could warm and rise again.

What Do You Think?

Octopuses are highly intelligent, complex creatures that can solve problems, store memories, emulate other animals, feel pain and even play. Unfortunately, these qualities are often ignored by people looking to capture, harm and kill them. Do you think people have the right to torture and kill octopuses just for sport or amusement? What do you think of the following activities?

OCTOPUS WRESTLING, ANYONE?

It might not be your idea of fun, but back in the 1950s and '60s, octopus wrestling was a fad. Over 100 participants attended the World Championships, which were held in Puget Sound, Washington, in 1963. Divers, some without breathing gear, dove down in shallow water, grappled with octopuses, and brought them to the surface. The divers who caught the biggest octopuses won the prizes. Over 5,000 people lined the shore to watch, and the event was televised. Caught octopuses were eaten, given to the local aquarium, or thrown back into the sea. Octopus wrestling is now illegal in Washington, but it's still being practised in certain circles.

OCTOPUS ON ICE

An octopus on ice in a fish market might not surprise you, but an octopus on the ice of a hockey rink might cause you to blink in disbelief. Back in 1952, the Detroit Red Wings started a tradition of throwing an octopus onto the ice when a couple of fans, who happened to be fishmonger brothers, tossed one into the middle of a game that the Red Wings finally won. (Why those guys took an octopus to a hockey game is anyone's guess.) Other fans liked the idea because they thought the eight arms symbolized the number of wins needed for a playoff victory, so they started to throw octopuses onto the ice before each game.

Today, it takes more than eight wins to carry home the Stanley Cup, but octopus-throwing has become a fad with fans of other US hockey teams, and the Louis Armstrong Arena even has octopuses hanging from the rafters. They are dead, but do you think it's necessary for these creatures to die just for our entertainment?

WHO EATS OCTOPUSES?

Several creatures feed on octopuses, including humans. Many people in countries around the world, including seafood gourmets right here at home, consider octopus to be a delicious treat. Spain and Portugal are known for gourmet dishes made from octopus. In Asian countries like Japan, Taiwan, Korea and China, octopus is a very popular everyday food.

If you saw "calamari" on a menu would you know what it was? This is an Italian word taken from a Greek word meaning "ink pot" for squid, the octopus's ink-squirting cousin. Calamari is prepared in much the same way as octopus, and served in many North American restaurants, as well as being a favourite in Mediterranean countries.

Octopuses have been caught since ancient times, using many methods. Some Greek fishermen still catch them the old-fashioned way—by lowering clay pots into the water. When an octopus crawls into a pot to hide, it's hauled up and taken home to cook.

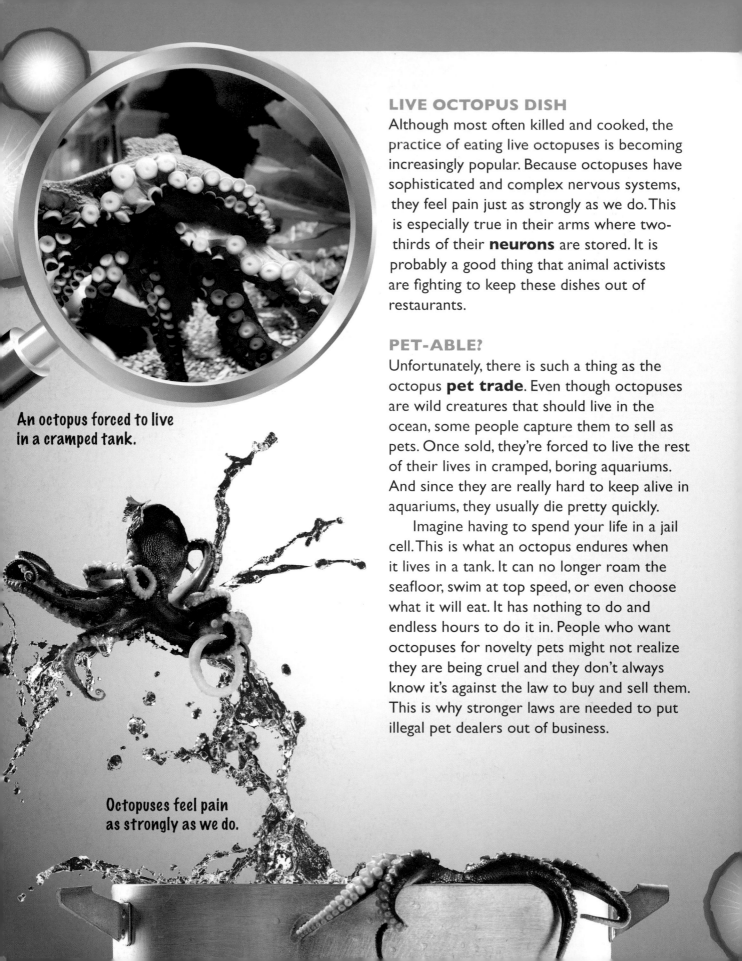

An octopus forced to live in a cramped tank.

Octopuses feel pain as strongly as we do.

LIVE OCTOPUS DISH

Although most often killed and cooked, the practice of eating live octopuses is becoming increasingly popular. Because octopuses have sophisticated and complex nervous systems, they feel pain just as strongly as we do. This is especially true in their arms where two-thirds of their **neurons** are stored. It is probably a good thing that animal activists are fighting to keep these dishes out of restaurants.

PET-ABLE?

Unfortunately, there is such a thing as the octopus **pet trade**. Even though octopuses are wild creatures that should live in the ocean, some people capture them to sell as pets. Once sold, they're forced to live the rest of their lives in cramped, boring aquariums. And since they are really hard to keep alive in aquariums, they usually die pretty quickly.

Imagine having to spend your life in a jail cell. This is what an octopus endures when it lives in a tank. It can no longer roam the seafloor, swim at top speed, or even choose what it will eat. It has nothing to do and endless hours to do it in. People who want octopuses for novelty pets might not realize they are being cruel and they don't always know it's against the law to buy and sell them. This is why stronger laws are needed to put illegal pet dealers out of business.

The media often portrays octopuses as scary, vicious monsters. But you've seen how they are actually intelligent, timid, and complex creatures. They possess a whole lot of interesting biological traits—they have blue blood and three hearts, and the ability to squirt ink, camouflage themselves and mimic other sea animals. From the biggest to the smallest, from the common to the most exotic, the variety of octopuses that live around the world is incredible.

Now that you've been in deep with octopuses, let's take another look at the quiz from page 8. Here are the answers:

What Do You Know?
Quiz Answers

1. **What is a radula?**
   It's something like a tongue covered with sandpaper that's strong enough to drill holes in shells.

2. **What does cephalopod mean?**
   It's a Greek name that means head-footed.

3. **What is melanin?**
   It's the stuff in an octopus's ink that also gives us our hair and skin colouring.

4. **Why is the greater blue-ringed octopus deadly?**
   It's the only octopus that could kill you with a bite.

5. **Why does an octopus have blue blood?**
   It has copper in its blood instead of the iron that makes our blood red.

6. **How does an octopus change directions?**
   Its siphon swings around like the nozzle of a hose.

7. **Does an octopus have any hard parts?**
   It has a hard, bony, parrot-like beak.

8. **How does an octopus prepare to eat a crab?**
   Its insides are turned to mush by the octopus's poisonous spit.

Are You Artistic?

How would you portray an octopus? Would you create a pencil sketch? A watercolour? An oil painting? Would you carve, sculpt, mold, or silk-screen? Would you use recycled soup tins?

Over the years, artists have used many materials on everything from totem poles to t-shirts to present their versions of octopuses. Their styles have run from realistic to "You mean that's supposed to be an *octopus*?"

QUICK CRAFTS
Make a Sock-topus

1. Find an old sock of any size. Make sure it doesn't have a hole in the toe.

2. Use paper or cloth scraps or a bunched-up plastic bag to roll into a ball and stuff into the toe of the sock.

3. Wrap a ribbon tightly beneath the ball and tie it with a bow. This will be the head of your octopus.

4. Cut the bottom part of the sock, just about up to the ribbon, into 8 even strips to make the octopus's arms.

5. Cut out two eye circles from white paper or felt. Give each eye a black pupil. Or if you have them available, use some googly eyes. Make a happy pink mouth if you wish.

6. Use a dab of glue to put the eyes and mouth in place—and presto!—you have a Sock-topus.

Try a Tube Octopus

1. Start with an empty toilet paper roll.

2. Make a ball of tissue paper and stuff it into one end of the roll, with the smooth surface on top.

3. Paint it any colour.

4. Cut two paper circles for eyes, and use a felt pen for pupils. If you have them available, use googly eyes instead. Glue on the eyes, and paint on a smile.

5. At the bottom of the toilet paper roll, cut 8 even strips about 5 cm (2 in) deep.

6. Roll up the 8 strips and your octopus is ready for duty as an ornament.

Glossary

BIPED is an animal that moves around on only two legs.

CEPHALOPOD is a group of molluscs, which includes octopuses, squids, nautiluses and cuttlefish.

CHITIN is the tough substance that forms the octopus's beak.

CHROMATOPHORES are pigment-containing cells that enable octopuses to change colours.

COPPER is the metal that makes octopus blood blue. It's also poisonous to octopuses.

CROP is a temporary storage area for partially digested food before it passes to the octopus's stomach.

ESOPHAGUS is the muscular tube that connects the throat to the stomach.

FALSE BODIES are small clouds of ink and mucous that octopuses squirt out to trick predators.

FOSSIL FUEL is fuel, such as coal, natural gas and oil, that humans use as their primary source of energy.

GILLS are respiratory organs that allow marine organisms to breathe under water.

GLOBAL WARMING is the rising temperature of the planet's oceans and atmosphere.

INVERTEBRATES are animals that don't have backbones.

IRON is the metal that makes human blood red.

KRILL is a type of zooplankton made of shrimp-type creatures, which is a major food source in the oceans.

MANTLE is the tissue covering the octopus's body.

MANTLE CAVITY is a watery space beneath the mantle that contains the gills and blood vessels.

MELANIN is a dark pigment found in skin, hair and octopus ink.

MOLLUSC is a division of invertebrates with soft bodies, and usually, hard shells.

NEURONS are cells that conduct nerve impulses and help us feel things like pain.

OVERFISHING is the act of fishing and catching too much of one species.

PET TRADE is the buying, selling or trading of animals.

PLANKTON is the collection of microscopic organisms, like algae, that drifts in the water.

RADULA is a flexible tongue-like organ covered in teeth used for scraping food.

SALINITY is the amount of salt in a body of water, like the ocean.

SECRETION is the release of a certain substance, like ink.

SIPHON is a tube-like structure on the mantle that pumps water and shoots ink.

SUCKER DISCS are muscular, flexible pads on an octopus's arms that help it grasp onto things.

TRAWLING is a type of commercial fishing where a trawl is dragged behind a boat to catch whatever it can grab.

Index

A
albino octopus, 21
arm, 11
Atlantic longarm octopus, 22, 24
Atlantic pygmy octopus, 22, 27

B
banded drop-arm octopus, 23
behaviour, 8, 11, 12, 13, 14, 16
big blue octopus, 22, 27
bite, 19
blanket octopus, 17, 23
blood, 8, 9

C
California Lilliput octopus, 20
camouflage, 14, 15, 17
Caribbean reef octopus, 22, 25
cephalopod, 8, 19, 37
chitin, 12, 37
chromatophore, 14, 17, 37
coconut octopus, 23, 25
colour. See camouflage
common octopus, 21, 23
copper, 9, 19, 37
crop, 9, 37
cruelty, 32-34
Cthulhu, 6

D
day octopus. See big blue octopus
deaf. See hearing
diet, 8, 10, 20
digestion, 9
Dumbo octopus, 22, 25

E
ears. See hearing
environmental threat, 28-29
esophagus, 9, 37
evolution, 10

F
false bodies, 14, 37
folklore, 7
four-eyed octopus, 22, 26

G
giant Pacific octopus, 20, 22, 23
gills, 9, 37
greater blue-ringed octopus, 8, 19

H
habitat, 16, 21, 22-23
hearing, 13
hearts, 9
hockey, 32-33
human consumption, 33-34

I
ink, 8, 9, 14
intelligence, 12, 19
invertebrate, 8, 37

K
krill, 29, 37

L
lifespan, 18

M
main brain, 9, 11
mantle, 9, 37
mantle cavity, 9, 37
mating, 16-18
melanin, 8, 14, 37
mimic octopus, 15
mini-brain, 9, 11
mollusc, 19, 37
mouth, 12
muscle. See strength

N
nerve poison, 19
neurons, 37
northern common octopus, 23, 24

O
octopus wrestling, 32
overfishing, 29, 37

P
Pacific Northwest tree octopus, 21
Paul the Prophesying Octopus, 7
pet trade, 34, 37
plankton, 10, 28, 37
predator, 9, 10

R
radula, 8, 12, 37

S
scent, 13
siphon, 9, 37
squid, 27
star-sucker pygmy octopus, 20
strength, 11
sucker disc, 11, 13, 37
swimming, 12

T
taste buds, 13
transparent pelagic octopus, 22, 24
trawling, 30, 37
Turquet's octopus, 22, 26, 31

V
vision, 13

W
wonderpus octopus, 21, 22

Further Reading

Banks, William. *Ollie the Octopus*. London: Safkhet Publishers, 2006.

Cerullo, Mary M. *The Octopus: Phantom of the Sea.* New York: Cobblehill Books 1997.

Hanlon, Roger. "Where's the Octopus?" *Science Friday*, 2011. Video.
http://www.sciencefriday.com/video/08/05/2011/where-s-the-octopus.html.

Keller, Holly. *An Octopus is Amazing*. New York: HarperCollins, 1991.

Markes, Julie. *Good Thing You're Not an Octopus!* New York: HarperCollins, 2006.

Most, Bernard. *My Very Own Octopus*. Boston: Houghton Mifflin Harcourt, 1991.

Rhodes, Mary Jo. *Undersea Encounters: Octopuses and Squids*. New York: Children's Press, 2005.

Bibliography

Anderson, Trevor, and Una McGovern. *Chambers Encyclopedia*. London: ChambersHarrap, 2001.

Fisheries and Oceans Canada. "Octopus by Dive Experimental Fishery - Pacific Region."
Fisheries and Oceans Canada. http://www.pac.dfo-mpo.gc.ca/fm-gp/commercial/
shellfish-mollusques/octopus-poulpe/index-eng.htm

Granite, Liz. "Species: Atlantic Longarm Octopus." *Everything Octopus*, March 22, 2009.
http://everythingoctopus.blogspot.ca/2009/03/species-atlantic-longarm-octopus.html.

Hanlon, Roger T. "Octopus Camouflage." Woods Hole Marine Biological Laboratory, 2009. Video.
Harmon, Katherine. "How Octopuses Make Themselves Invisible," *Scientific American*.
June 1, 2012. http://blogs.scientificamerican.com/octopus-chronicles/2012/06/01/
how-octopuses-make-themselves-invisible.

Hanlon, Roger T., and John B. Messenger. *Cephalopod Behavior*. Cambridge: Cambridge University
Press, 1998.

Landman, Neil H., Richard Arnold Davis, and Royal H. Mapes, eds. *Cephalopods Past and Present:
New Insights and Fresh Perspectives*. Dordrecht: Springer, 2007.

Mather, Jennifer A., James B. Wood and Roland C. Anderson. Octopus: *The Ocean's Intelligent
Invertebrate*. Portland: Timber Press, 2010.

Monterey Bay Aquarium Research Institute. "DeepSee Discovers Rare Pelagic Octopus."
Undersea Hunter. http://www.underseahunter.com/n28/
deepsee-discovers-rare-pelagic-octopus.html.

Pappas, Stephanie. "Clever Octopus Mimics a Fish." *Live Science*, March 4, 2010.
http://www.livescience.com/6153-clever-octopus-mimics-fish.html.

Strugnell, Jan. *Turquet's Octopus and Antarctic Warming*. Melbourne: La Trobe University Press, 2012.

Image Credits